Joe Meig

Reflections on the Game

Joseph J. Geiger

Illustrated by Anna Dvorak

To the kid, young or old, who loves the game of basketball.

Table of Contents

The reward of a thing well done, is to have done it.

Ralph Waldo Emerson

Introduction

Over a century ago, Dr. James A. Naismith unknowingly set into motion the concept that would evolve into the sport most played in America. By nailing a peach basket to the wall of a gymnasium in Springfield, Massachusetts in 1891, he created the great game of basketball. Though the peach basket has been replaced by fiberglass and steel, everyone that plays the game shares in its competitive spirit. From those with great physical abilities to those with mental and physical handicaps, basketball is played at all levels and by people of all ages.

Basketball Joe takes a refreshing look at this great game and the players that participate at its purest level—high school. It is a time when your teammates are the kids you grow up with and your childhood dreams can still become reality. It is a place where smoking and drinking are prohibited and the influence of media and money have not been allowed to exploit the players. But most importantly, it is a period of goal-setting, physical and mental development, and self-discovery.

On the surface, *Basketball Joe* is a scrapbook of words and illustrations depicting many of the feelings and experiences shared by high school players. But it also serves as a guide for successful living. In basketball, as in life, the issues of self-confidence, discipline, hard work, and persistence emerge in the conflict between the mind's desire to succeed and our inner ability to achieve.

Though *Basketball Joe* attempts to bridge the sport of basketball with the broader lessons of life, it is also meant to be enjoyed—like the game. So whether you are at home, in the library, or on a park bench, just set your basketball down, loosen your sneakers and relax. For the next hour or so, take a journey with me through the greatest game of all, high school basketball.

Chapter One

Why We Play

The grand essentials to happiness in this life are something to do, something to love and something to hope for.

Joseph Addison

Because of its accessibility, virtually all can share in the enjoyment the game of basketball offers. But one thing is certain, the dedicated ball player is drawn to the game. There is something about basketball that touches the soul. It becomes more than just a game. It becomes a vehicle that can elevate you and make you a better person. It gives you a purpose, a positive route to which you can devote yourself and your talents and know that what you put in will be returned many times over.

Enjoyment

Any kid that picks up a basketball and heads out under a driveway flood light can tell you what a great experience it is.

The calm, quiet sounds of a warm summer night are interrupted only by the bouncing of the ball, the shuffling of feet, and swish of the net. Adrenaline pumps through your veins as you break into a comfortable sweat. With the extra spring in your step and snap in your jumper, everything seems to go a little more smoothly. With nothing to distract you, the dreams of championship games and last second heroics fill your mind.

The serenity of the evening and the oneness with the game make you feel so alive and your dreams so worthwhile.

Competition

What lies behind us and what lies in front of us are tiny matters compared to what lies within us.

Ralph Waldo Emerson

It's that competitive spirit inside of you that motivates you, forcing you to push yourself, constantly testing your skills. It is that love of a battle, that excitement of a new challenge that fuels your drive to compete.

Competition is playing your brother one-on-one. Loser mows the lawn.

Outlet

Games lubricate the body and the mind.

Benjamin Franklin

Basketball offers you a pressure valve from everyday life. It gives you the opportunity to clear your mind of your problems, relieve yourself of your anxieties, and sort things out. Although your problems will not disappear by themselves, after a hard work-out and hot shower, they never seem to be as serious.

Achievement

We judge ourselves by what we feel capable of doing, while others judge us by what we have already done.

Henry Wadsworth Longfellow

Being a dedicated basketball player, you are always focusing on the future. Never content with your past accomplishments, you judge yourself on your progress, your dedication, and your ability to perform. This year you made the starting line up, next year you want to become All-Conference.

There are no parameters that surround achievement. It must be defined by each individual. Only you know when you have truly achieved.

Recognition

Public life is the crown of a career, and to the young man it is the worthiest of all ambitions.

Lord Tweedsmuir

Dating back to ancient Greece, our society has had a fascination with sports and the athletes who compete in them. We love to watch athletes compete as we admire their talents, instincts, and ability to perform under pressure. We love to put the victors on pedestals and shower them with praise. To a youngster, this type of recognition is very real and very powerful.

The Game

Like our heroes that went before us, now it is our time to make our mark in the record books.

The game is a time for your basketball dreams to become reality, and the court is the stage where they are played out. When you step out onto the court, nothing else seems to matter. For thirty-two minutes the world stands still while you do what you enjoy doing the most....playing basketball.

Chapter Two

The Early Years

You are never given a wish without also being given the power to make it come true. You may have to work at it, however.

Richard Bach, <u>Illusions</u>

Striving for excellence is difficult and often frustrating. As we work to reach new levels of expertise, we are constantly being bombarded with new challenges. Just when that right-handed lay-up is finally perfected, you need to work on the left hand. We allow ourselves little time to be content with our level of play. There is always another skill to be mastered.

The Driveway

Someone, somewhere is practicing right now.

Drive down any country road or city street and you will find that common trio of kid, ball and basket. Whether it is a driveway, hayloft, schoolyard, or barnyard, they all represent the same thing. It is a retreat, a place where you can get away and work on your game. There you develop a feel for the game, playing against man's toughest opponent, Mother Nature.

You are the kid shooting baskets with mittens on after a fifteen inch snowfall. You are the kid with the sweat-drenched body playing in the sweltering city heat of a summer afternoon. You are the soaking wet figure shooting around before school on a misty fall morning.

It is during these times that a lot of thinking takes place and a lot of dreams take hold. It is here that you establish a course that will take you beyond the mediocre basketball player.

Summer Camp

Don't teach kids plays, teach them how to play.

Bobby Knight

Basketball camps are the perfect opportunity for you to learn the basics of this simple game. Anyone or any team that tries to turn it into a game of complex formulas and fancy plays is only making it more difficult.

Attending basketball camp will not automatically make you a better player. It should, however, teach you the fundamentals necessary to become one.

Your Style

...Style is the man.

Comte de Buffon

Like the woodcarver sculpting a figure out of a block of wood, you carve your style out of the God-given talents you possess. Every time you go down in your basement to practice your ball-handling, to the gym to shoot around, or the weight room to work on your strength, you are refining old skills and developing new ones. During this process of chopping, whittling, and shaving, certain trademark qualities begin to emerge, defining your game and creating your unique style.

Gym Rat

By failing to prepare, you are preparing to fail.

Benjamin Franklin

Two of the most important things you can do when you first get to high school are get acquainted with the librarian and the janitor. The librarian opens the door to the adventures of Huck Finn, the wisdom of Thomas Jefferson, and the courage of Abraham Lincoln. The janitor opens the door to the gym.

Makeshift Hoops

There is nothing more valuable to a young man on a rainy day than his imagination.

As the cold rain beats against the window, you sit on your bed molding your latest creation. Using a clothes hanger, mesh potato sack, a roll of tape, and a balled up pair of athletic socks, you are supplied with entertainment for hours...or at least until something breaks.

Dunk Ball

Technology may have unlocked the mysteries of flight, but the dream to fly still lives in the hearts of fledgling basketball stars around the world.

The time-worn wheels of the machine-shed door squeal as they slide along the track. While one guy turns on the lights, another jumps into the cab of the John Deere tractor and backs it out past the nine foot hoop. Another grabs a broom and begins sweeping the shed floor, exposing the court.

For hours you and your buddies play dunk ball in the dusty old shed. Fantasies become reality as you are able to duplicate the great plays you see on T.V.; throwing ally-oops, hanging on the rim, goal tending, pinning lay-ups against the backboard.

A good, fast-paced, action packed game of dunk ball always leaves you wondering just how good you could be. If you were only a foot taller.

Chapter Three

What It Takes

Ability is only a small percentage of what determines an athlete's success. Desire, a high threshold of pain, pride of the right kind so that you are never satisfied, are what makes the difference. You can't be satisfied or you'll stop improving.

Tom Osborn

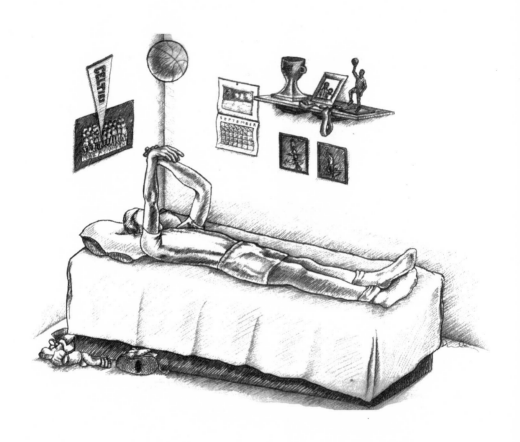

Dreams

(Athletes) demonstrate the scope of human possibility,
which is unlimited. The inconceivable is conceived, and
then is accomplished.

Brian Glanville

You lie in your bed, dreaming of the great feats you will someday accomplish. Images of last-second heroics and post-game interviews fill your mind. Everyone has hopes and dreams of things they would like to accomplish. The sad thing is, too many people ignore them, believing they are foolish or unattainable. What you must realize is that your dreams are the compass of your heart. They give you direction, telling you where you want to go, what you wish to be, and what you hope to accomplish. Don't let the mere challenge of a dream intimidate you. Take a chance and follow your heart, for all great things start as dreams.

Goal-den Rules

If you want to be happy, set a goal that commands your thoughts, liberates your energy, and inspires your hopes.

Andrew Carnegie

1) Your goals are a guide that tell you in which direction to go. Dream big, set high goals. If you fall short you still have achieved great things.

2) Ralph Waldo Emerson said, "Man becomes what he thinks about all day long." Write your goals down, and put them in a place where you will see them daily.

3) Break up your larger goals into smaller goals. This makes them seem less overwhelming and gives you a greater sense of achievement along the way.

4) Make yourself a road map. Outline a series of steps to achieving goals and evaluate yourself often. What are your strengths? What do you need to work on? Anthony Robbins says, "Goals are dreams with a deadline."

5) Be sure you are willing to make the sacrifices necessary to succeed. If you do not enjoy the climb, the peak will not be worth it.

How to be a Champion

You wonder how they do it and you look to see the knack.

You watch the foot in action, or the shoulder, or the back.

But when you spot the answer where the higher glamours lurk,

You'll find in moving higher up the laurel covered spire,

That most of it is practice and the rest of it is work.

Grantland Rice

Hard Work

Without dreams there is no need to work. Without work there is no need to dream.

Anonymous

Dreaming may be where achievement begins, but hard work is where it is attained. Without sweat there is no hope for your dreams to materialize. Hard work puts dreams in motion, giving them a chance to become reality.

There is no substitute for hard work.

Discipline

I've never known a man worth his salt who in the long run, deep down in his heart, didn't appreciate the grind, the discipline. There is something in good men that really yearns for discipline.

Vince Lombardi

Discipline is...

Doing the little things... execution... tedious drills... annoying lectures... moving your feet... making free throws... taking a charge... blocking out... weak-side help... knowing when to take it in... when to kick it out... when to hold it up... when to say "yes"... when to say "no"... when not to say anything at all.

Discipline is the process of molding an athlete into a more controlled and effective basketball player.

Persistence

I am not discouraged, because every wrong attempt discarded is another step forward.

Thomas Edison

Persistence is the opposite of all at once. It means sticking with something, not giving up, and not losing hope in the fact that your hard work will pay off. Persistence offers the less talented individual, who desires to excel, compensation for his lack of natural ability. God did not give every person the same amount of talent. But God did give each of us an endless supply of potential and the tools to develop it.

Luck

The harder we work, the luckier we get.

George Allen

You've practiced that shot a thousand times. Now you finally make one when it counts and everyone calls it luck.

99 Straight

We are what we repeatedly do. Excellence, then, is not an act, but a habit.

Aristotle

You can remember that feeling the first time you made fifty free throws in a row... the machine-like fashion in which you executed it.

Your elbow acted like a hinge every time you followed through, the ball popping the net and slowly bouncing back. You think to yourself, "If I can make fifty in a row I can make a hundred."

It's the gratification you receive from achieving the smaller goals and reaching new plateaus that fuels your ego with hope and confidence, assuring you that your dreams are in the process of coming true.

Attitude

Attitude is the father of action.

Author Unknown

It was the bad call by the official, the wrong decision by the coach, a teammate's mistake, the size of the gym, too much air in the ball, or a floor that was too slippery. You can always find an excuse when something goes wrong. But that's not your style. You accept things the way they are and move on. You know that excuses and blame are only a sign of weakness. In taking responsibility for your own mistakes, you mature and develop, reaching your full potential.

You can't always control the outcome of every situation. But you can control your response.

Chapter Four

The People Involved

The two things that will most influence your life in the next five years are the people you meet and the books you read.

Lou Holtz

Role Models

Without heroes, we are all plain people and don't know
how far we can go.

Bernard Malamud

It might be a family member, a neighbor, a local high school player, or your favorite NBA star. It doesn't matter. If your role model possesses the qualities you admire, he or she symbolizes a visual road map of what you wish to become. His or her actions inspire and direct you, teaching you how to live and react to life's obstacles.

Choose your role models carefully: you are destined to follow in their footsteps.

The Coach

Through sports, a coach offers a boy a way to sneak up on the mysteries of manhood.

Author Unknown

His impact is far more reaching than merely teaching the fundamentals and strategies of the game. Through his direction and support he helps you establish a foundation for success, one of vision, discipline, hard work, and integrity. It is this foundation that prepares you not only for game time, but a lifetime as well.

The Chemistry of a Coach

Teacher... Dreamer... Motivator... Communicator... Decision maker... Disciplinarian... Counselor... Strategist... Manager... Leader... Guardian... Role Model... Friend.

Teammates

...To get the full value of joy you must have somebody to divide it with.

Mark Twain

A basketball team is a cohesive group of individuals bonded together by the common goal of winning. Skin color, social status, intellectual ability and outside interests are of no importance on the court. What does matter is your capacity to contribute to the team. Every player has his role. Certain jobs require a lot of responsibility with great reward while others call for a big commitment with little recognition. Regardless of your role, it is unselfish commitment to the betterment of the team that is most important. There is no "I" in "team".

Parents

We never know the love of the parents until we become parents ourselves.

Henry Ward Beecher

It is a comforting feeling to know that your parents are in the crowd. Teaching you that you can be anything you want to be, they work hard to make your dreams possible. As your #1 fans, they drive you to practice, send you to camps, and allow you time to develop your skills. Their love and sacrifice never runs out. Following your career from start to finish, they are happy when you are up, sad when you are down, and always proud.

The Fans

I never saw a game without taking sides and never want to see one. There is the soul of the game.

Warren G. Harding

The crowd has a far-reaching effect on the game of basketball. With the potential to elevate an athlete's performance, intimidate opponents, and influence officials, it's no wonder they call it "the sixth man."

A game brings a scattered community together to form a tightly knit crowd and helps make basketball such a pure event.

The Officials

Officiating is the only occupation in the world where the highest accolade is silence.

Earl Strom

The official stands at the baseline awaiting the end of a time-out when a voice coming from the visitor's section yells, "It's a great game, Ref. You really should try and watch a little more of it." Another voice battles back from the home side, "Ref, you're doing a great job, keep it up." Yet this allegiance may last only as long as the next whistle.

The game is not perfect and neither are its officials, but they do play an essential role in bringing control and sanity to organized basketball.

Fall Ball

You always know that with the start of a new school year, fall is close behind. To most people it means cool evenings, early sunsets, rustling leaves, and Friday night football games. But it also means a new basketball season is right around the corner.

As the pre-season picks begin to circulate, anticipation and excitement begin to mount. You look to the shelter of a warm gymnasium to complete the final touches of your game.

It won't be long now before the cold winds of winter will be blowing, and you will be hearing the familiar sounds of squeaky tennis shoes and the coach's whistle.

Chapter Five

The Price We Pay

The universe is so vast and so ageless that the life of one man can only be justified by the measure of his sacrifice.

Pilot Officer V.A. Rosewarne

Practice

The best thing about basketball is the opportunity to prove your greatness as a team.

Pat Riley

As you stand on the endline waiting the start of another conditioning drill, you are reminded that practice is a whole new ball game from the wide-open free-style game of the summer. Here, mental and physical transitions begin to take place, roles are defined, and the team's game plan starts to emerge.

Defeat

Yet each struggle, each defeat, sharpens your skills and strengths, your courage and endurance, your ability and your confidence, and thus each obstacle is a comrade-in-arms forcing you to become better... or quit.

Og Mandino

Defeat always marks the end... the end of a game, the end of a season, the end of a dream. It is in defeat that you are forced to ask yourself, "Where do I go from here?" Ralph Waldo Emerson said, "Our greatest glory consists not in never failing, but in rising every time we fall." It is with this attitude that you turn defeat not into an end, but a beginning. This gives you the opportunity to bounce back from adversity, develop a new game plan, and return ready to fight a new battle.

Fatigue

It is better to wear out than rust out.

Author Unknown

The lactic acid builds up in your muscles, your body gets tired, and your mind becomes clouded. You push yourself mentally and physically until you do not think you can go any further. Then you dig a little deeper, fight a little harder, and you find you can.

Time

Do not squander time, for that's the stuff life is made of.

Benjamin Franklin

The time commitment required for a successful basketball season is extensive. During the off-season you spend time at camps, clinics, leagues, open gym, and daily workouts. Throughout the season it is the time spent at after school practice, Saturday morning scrimmages, holiday tournaments, and night games that consume your leisure hours.

In this day of high-tech computers, fast-food restaurants and get-rich-quick schemes, time seems to be the forgotten sacrifice of excellence. You learn through athletics, however, that it takes time to learn, develop, and ultimately succeed. And because high school athletics come only once in a lifetime, it is time well-spent.

Injury

There is no defense for the unexpected.

Basketball is a game of running, jumping, starting, stopping, bumping, falling, pushing, and twisting. Every time you step on the court you are susceptible to injury. Although you are never fully prepared for this setback, good conditioning may help prevent an injury from occuring.

Embarrassment

Embarrassment is to the mind what dizziness is to the body.

Ludwig Borne.

Every time we step into the spotlight there lies the potential for embarrassment. Getting the ball stolen, missing a wide open lay-up, shooting an air ball or getting your shot blocked are all humiliating experiences. Whether it strikes a confident young superstar or a tentative inexperienced substitute, the feelings are the same. No one wants to be embarrassment's next victim.

Frustration

When you get to the end of your rope, tie a knot and hang on.

Franklin Roosevelt

While habits respond to training, emotions don't. Some days no matter how hard you try, nothing seems to go right. In your frustration you find yourself doing things you really don't like doing, such as arguing with your teammates, kicking the bench, or yelling at the officials. On the basketball court, where pride is always up for grabs, it is easy to get frustrated in the heat of a competitive battle. As you begin to grow and mature as a player you develop a composure that allows you to channel your energies into your game. It is this poise that separates the average player from the great one.

In The Groove

Basketball is a game of rhythm. The only way you're going to get that rhythm is by repetition. You do a thing a thousand times and pretty soon you do it easily and gracefully.

Adolph Rupp

It can all start with a couple of great plays back-to-back. You hit a jump shot, make a great pass, and soon you are influencing the rhythm of the game. The ball starts to feel like an extension of your arm. Everything you put up goes in. Confidence is high and you want the ball. The other team tries to make adjustments by switching defensive players on you, but it does no good. You are already in the groove.

Chapter Six

The Pay We Prize

The years teach much which the days never know.

Ralph Waldo Emerson

Tournament Time

Life is not dated merely by years. Events are sometimes the best calenders.

Benjamin Franklin

Just as the cold winds of winter welcome the season, it is only fitting that the early signs of spring escort it out. Every year in March the regular season winds down and the regional rankings fall into place. All-Conference, All-District and All-State selections are made and conference champions are crowned.

The excitement surrounding high school basketball in March is contagious. It is the time of the year when the spirit of the tournament spills out of the teams and into their communities. Store owners close up shop and businesses shut down as townspeople go out to support their teams. Thousands of people make their annual pilgrimage to the high school state tournaments. Memories of teams and heroes past are dusted off and discussed. Old records fall as new ones are established.

For the player, there is nothing like it. This is the pinnacle of high school basketball. Every young kid who dreams and prepares to excel in high school basketball hopes of playing in the state tournament. The crowds, cameras, and big arenas are what it is all about. Winning the state tournament is the dream of every young team.

Victory

There is no substitute for victory.

Douglas MacArthur

Winning is the remedy for all team problems. It affects how you perceive yourself and your teammates. When your team is winning, there is never any blame or anger directed at anyone. Practice is more enjoyable, school is more interesting, and you look forward to games with more anticipation. Morale is high and team unity is strong.

In our society where being number one is so coveted, winning makes it all worthwhile. To be victorious; that is why we keep score.

Character

Life is like a grindstone, whether it wears you out or shines you up depends on what you are made of.

Author Unknown

You can feel it the second the ball leaves your hand. The free throw —with one second left on the clock to send the game into overtime — falls short. It is during a defining moment like this that you are forced to make a decision. Do you decide that you are a choker or do you put it behind you and look forward to the next game-winning opportunity for redemption? By choosing to move on, you do not let the disappointment of a temporary setback detract from what you have already accomplished. This is what character is all about.

Confidence

Experience tells you what to do; confidence allows you to do it.

Author Unknown

Confidence is believing in yourself and your abilities. It comes from practice, practice, and more practice. Through repetition you develop strength and consistency which enhances your performance level. This, in turn, increases your confidence, so that your choices are no longer filled with doubt and hesitation, but the natural flow of your instincts.

Confidence says, "Give me the ball when it counts."

Leadership

The greatest thing in this world is not so much where we are, but in which direction we are moving.

Author Unknown

Being a leader is more than wearing the title of Team Captain. A leader is someone who sets the pace for the whole team. He is the individual who establishes the team work ethic and vision. He is the player that the team looks to in game situations to keep it poised and under control. By carving out a positive course for himself, a leader naturally gains the respect of others. And by maintaining this course, others will follow.

Sportsmanship

It's not true that nice guys finish last. Nice guys are winners before the game even begins.

Author Unknown

According to the scoreboard, every game has winners and losers. But when the final buzzer sounds, there is a lot to be learned about the competitors from both benches.

It is common knowledge that we all must learn how to deal with defeat. Much less is said about the need to learn how to win. As in the sorrow of defeat, the exhilaration of victory calls for self control. One of the most admirable qualities in the character of a true winner is his quiet confidence and ability to remain humble and gracious in both victory and defeat.

There is nothing that proves good sportsmanship makes you a better athlete; but it does make you a classier one.

Memories

That it will never come again is what makes life so sweet.

Emily Dickinson

When the last buzzer of the final game sounds and the day comes to hang up the old jersey, a door closes behind us. Unable to return to that time, all we are able to take with us are the glorified memories of days gone by. These memories are carried with us wherever we go, forever impacting and enriching our lives. They give us all the opportunity to become legends in our own minds.

Contribution

*You can't live a perfect day without doing something for
someone who will never be able to repay you.*

John Wooden

I still enjoy shooting baskets on a quiet summer evening. It gives me time
to relax and unwind after a long day. Sometimes I think back on my high
school years, what I put into them and what I gained in return. I think
about the people I met along the way, the friendships I developed, and the
guidance I received. There were so many people who took the time and
energy to work with me and teach me this great game. Like them, I feel an
obligation to pass the game on to future generations. Whether it is through
coaching, volunteering time to a summer rec program, or playing one-on-
one with the youngster down the street, sharing my love of basketball is
mutually rewarding. You never know what words of wisdom or
encouragement may start a dream rolling.

About the author

Joe Geiger learned the game of basketball growing up in the countryside of South central Minnesota. He worked hard enough on his game to help lead his high school basketball team to the Minnesota State Basketball tournament. He was also honored as one of five finalists for the 1984 Mr. Basketball of Minnesota award.

Today, Joe works as a financial consultant in New Prague, Minnesota. He and his wife Angela are kept busy raising three young hoopsters of their own; Joe Jr., Andrew, and Johnathan.

Acknowledgements

Throughout my playing days and during the process of writing *Basketball Joe,* many people were influencial. I would like to thank my parents Leroy and Jean who have always been there for me, my two brothers Duane and Ron who are outstanding role models as well as my two sisters Lorie and Julie for their support. I would also like to thank Brad Schoenbauer, Mary Kamish, Anna Dvorak, Dave Kamish, Todd Fultz, Art Gorgan, Pat Quinn, my teammates and coaches, especially Merv Sheplee for the countless hours he has dedicated to the game.

Finally, I would like to thank my loving wife Angela and my three sons Joey, Drew and Johnathan for their time and patience for without it this book would have never been completed.